IGNITE

Ignite

Rona Shaffran

George Payerle, Editor

Signature Editions

Cover design by Doowah Design.
Photo of Rona Shaffran by Alan Dean Photography.

This book was printed on Ancient Forest Friendly paper.
Printed and bound in Canada by Hignell Book Printing Inc.

We acknowledge the support of The Canada Council for the Arts and the Manitoba Arts Council for our publishing program.

Library and Archives Canada Cataloguing in Publication

Shaffran, Rona
Ignite / Rona Shaffran.

Poems.
ISBN 978-1-927426-02-9

I. Title.

PS8637.H34I35 2013 C811'.6 C2013-900985-X

Signature Editions
P.O. Box 206, RPO Corydon, Winnipeg, Manitoba, R3M 3S7
www.signature-editions.com

for Brian

. . . and let our bodies lose all
their loneliness.

—from "The Nude Swim"
Anne Sexton

Table of Contents

I

II

III

I

In the long journey out of the self,
There are many detours, washed-out interrupted raw places
Where the shale slides dangerously
And the back wheels hang almost over the edge
At the sudden veering, the moment of turning.

—from "Journey to the Interior"
Theodore Roethke

Burnt Forest

Their kisses taut
and parched

for so many
years now,

she chanced it, lips parted
full on his mouth,

his lips closed, their suppleness
a taunting

reminder
of sweetness past.

He turned back
to his book,

neck muscles stitched
and bound.

It was then
she remembered

the black, burnt trees
by the highway,

standing like spears
in lush green fields.

Chaste

Winter moon
streams through the window
electroplating our bedcovers,

squares of light silver
your face, a death mask
silent as the crusted snow.

In a stinging wind,

the nearby streetlamp combs
our front yard for shadows,

a broken white umbrella limps
down the monochrome street.

A metal street sign strikes
its steel post,

clanging
the tocsin bell.

Impasse

1

Skin
moist
from the bath,
I wait
on the landing
in nothing
but slippers.

Even to me
I smell female
and ripe.

You climb the stairs,
extolling the sleekness
of your new
navy Nubuck shoes,

then complain
about all you didn't fulfil
at the office today.

You scan my body
as though looking
for an answer
and say,

I forgot
to pay
the electric today.

2

Home, finally, after rain, teeming,
traffic, dizzying,
street lights, fractured.

Front door jammed, to enter
I had to shove hard
against its swollen seal.

My day's only triumph:
buying these navy Nubucks
I had coveted so long.

Climbing the stairs, raving
about my shoes, recounting
my bitter
day,

I notice
the double scallop
of your hips
as you stand
there on the landing,

your wedge of dark curls
a challenge
I just can't
seem to face.

Early Morning Mist

Amber fields scuttle away
and crouch in tall mist.

Trees angular
as a runic alphabet
line the roadside,

their naked
limbs reach
into nothing.

I'm driving myself… where?

One touch
                    one touch

Unseen

You sit at our kitchen table —
the morning paper.

Thinning hair on the crown
of your head
describes a small circle.

Tonsure.

I almost stroke it,
your scalp, virginal,
imagine it pliant
under my fingers.

But, last night I walked
unclothed into our room,
and you looked
through my nakedness,

like so many other times,
my flesh
retracting
under your absent stare.

My love churns
like a river in winter,
unseen under ice,
although I feel my bridges
shaking.

A freezing stays
my hand.

Manna: a prayer

Alone in the street, after an icy rain,
she cranes her neck, puzzled
by what appear to be black knobs
high on the branches
of a bare ash,

when, as if on cue,
all the knobs explode
into an aerial parabola alive
with black-capped chickadees

which alight on a cherry bush beside her,
the bush trembling, the flock gorging
on garnet berries
boxed in glinting ice.

She races to gather
the half-eaten
skins, rain of ruby crystals
in her cupped and grateful palms.

Unclothed

They undress back to back
by the bedroom hamper
and shimmy past each other
down the narrow hallway
to prepare for bed.

She washes up at her sink,
he at his,
their two vanities divided.

When he reaches for a towel,
his arm grazes
her right breast.

Her wet left hand reflexes
to touch the breast
where his ready lips
once hungered.

He turns away,
then pivots, reminding
himself to kiss her.

Their teeth clash
through half-clenched
lips.

Night's Corridor

She lies beside him, the rhythm
of his breath at odds with hers,
as she slips into sleep's corridor,

where cut-glass doors with crystal handles
open to glass-walled rooms mirroring
all the moments of their lives.

At the hallway's start, wedding bands
glimmer in the heart's silver chamber
as he rushes to embrace her
at first hint of her tears.

Mid-passage, a maze of rearview mirrors reflect
shared breakfasts and plans for the upcoming day.
In the blind spot, his absent morning bulge,
her wayward wetness, their modest kiss good-bye.

At the far end of the hallway, outside
their bedroom door, two concave mirrors
turn face to face.

Glass shatters,
a thousand stings.

Impact

1

A staccato
pelting rain
wakes her.

She nudges him,
pats his dormant
sex, whispering

Come over
to me.

Groggy *hmmm*
in reply.

I can take a hint,
she sighs.

What hint?
he asks.

2

His words tangle
around her
like a frayed blanket.

She throws back the covers,
sits up in bed,
plants her feet on the floor,

walks toward the shower,
lifts off her nightie
in front of the mirror,

pausing
to take in her nakedness:

impact of searching breasts,
ribs tapered toward scoop
of hips, rounded abdomen
and still, dark groin.

3

As hot water kneads her muscles,
a lover, long-gone, nuzzles.
She unhooks
the shower hose,

directs it to her most exquisite fold,
her breasts swell, a flood
of heat churns her gut,

she presses her body
against the cool white tiles,
squeezing out tears that mingle
with the chute of water.

4

The rain chills as it falls
icestorm sealing
their bedroom
window.

An Opening

A recurrent gnawing,
this ache of abstinence,

until one night, her need
unquenchable, endless,

she draws her thigh against his softparts,
their slow motility against her skin,

but avoidance has become his body's habit
too, he kisses her breasts, tenderly, cuddles
her head to his chest, drifts into dreamless

sleep. Stretched out awake, she senses
her desire open
into a long corridor, beyond
where he could go.

Cracks

In the backyard near midnight,
she unties her bathrobe.

Particles of moonlight drench
her face, trickle between her breasts,

converge in her groin
and run down her thighs,

cool quicksilver pooling
between her toes.

The porcelain moon
cracks —

she drops the bathrobe
and falls to her knees.

City Limits

Slamming
her car door shut,
she pulls out
of the driveway,

night's tattered leash
tightening
around her
with every passing mile.

On the highway,
just beyond city limits,
an image lifts through fog:

a russet stag stares directly at her,
monumental
in the headlights' frank gaze,

an intelligent face
with deep-set eyes bespeaking
power of the loins

to change her life.

The creature pivots like Nureyev
and vanishes into the far
heart of the forest,

smoky white birch,
moss-supple earth,

leaving her
to yearn.

Three

The streets empty
into violet twilight,
a few last shoppers
at the corner market.

A woman, narrow-faced,
waits ahead of me in line:
no makeup,
chestnut hair greying
at the temples, her fingers
long, ringless.

She arranges her choices
in a neat row
for the checkout girl —

one lemon,
one fat-free yogurt,
one grain-fed chicken breast,

one bag of baby spinach
enough
for three meals

for one,
who could be
me.

Light: a prayer

The sky buttoned
with ashen clouds,
slicing cold,

steam curling
from sewers,
from scarf-covered mouths.

People rush by,
heads bowed, eyes downcast,
foreheads creased

when, all at once,
in a hedge along the sidewalk,
three rufous-sided towhees

chirp
an ebullient chorus,

kyrie to a sudden
incandescence of sunlight
on cedar branches.

Improbable

Like a loose tooth
their union
dangles by threads,
painful when pushed,
ready to snap,
improbably hanging on.

Trapped

The young couple dance
among our guests,
sparks of starlight flash
in their eyes.

We carve precise circles
on careful feet,
wearing public smiles.

Our eyes search
the distant wall.

Erosion

At the river, the wind snarls
above clumps of bleached grass.

Sky looms.

She quickens
her step, pulls her coat close, turns

her face
to a glassy-eyed sun,

blinding waves
eroding the shore.

In the Rain

Alone in London,
walking in the rain
among flowing ranks of strangers,

I encounter a tall man,
his hair thick and black,
his coat grey flannel.

As we pass each other,
our eyes hold
for a moment.

We continue, in different
directions
but not indifferent.

Twenty years later,
why do I see his face
walking in the rain?

Suspended

Pungent yet sweet:
crushed
balsam needles
perfume November's rain.

This moment
hangs like beads of water
suspended along the rim
of a glass table.

A crow caws —
the moment
snaps.

Salve

Stretched to fracture
on the procrustean bed
of her life
(the lulls apprehensive,
the respites transient)

her heart remembers early
morning cool in Ecuador,
its long-ago caress still
tender on her skin

ENTREATY

My body is string,
unknot me

My body is elastic,
snap me

My body is quicksilver,
contain me

My body is a mango,
peel me

My body is a postage stamp,
lick me

My body is fresh-baked bread,
so butter me

Lullaby

A straw-coloured tom,
his golden fur knotted by rain,
huddles against the red brick
of the house, face scarred and wary.

I stop, reach out, but he flicks claws at me,
then later that night stares hard
at the blue bowl of milk I bring him.

Every night I carry
the blue bowl of milk to him
like a plea to the stony gods
of this forlorn year,

until one twilight
he deigns to drink
and I dare
to stroke him.

After, he roams our house,
I bathe him in warm water,
untangle his wet fur,
wrap him in a wool blanket.

He claims a spot
by the heat vent
and purrs me
a low lullaby.

Shifting

Vast bales of cloud billow
across a lightless sky.

The wind
shifts,

layers peel away
like a lover's clothes

to reveal the moon,
its glowing flesh.

PLUNGE

She waits for him, the street
bitter and wet, her shoulder
weighted low
by a briefcase of duty.

He pulls up alongside the curb:
she slides in, the click
of her seatbelt
a chain-link gate slammed shut.

They rush into urgent briefing —
dinner plans, groceries, phone
calls, what bills need paying
when

~

She gazes
out the window,

hears the gasp
of circus crowds

as her partner swings
by his knees

on the trapeze below,
arched to catch her.

She grabs the high trapeze bar, springs
from the platform, swings

forward, back over the pedestal board
and forward again,

releases
the bar

and plunges
through air

II

They cried,
"Ohoyaho,
Ohoo" …
Celebrating the marriage
Of flesh and air.

—from "Life is Motion"
Wallace Stevens

Small Island

1

A small island waits
as minutes, hours, years
slip into the surf.

Impelled
by the winds,
I travel there.

As my boat pulls near, a silent volcano
rears from the cobalt sea
to beckon me, its slopes surging
across the island, cleaving
the land in two.

A narrow road swoops
down to the sea, coiling
and uncoiling, past steep inclines
spiked with cacti, thick
with twisted olive trees and ferns.
Caper vines meander
across lavarock terraces.

In the village, stucco houses
tinted ochre and peach
clasp the volcano, float
amid fuchsia. Lemon
and wild fennel
spice the afternoon air.

The church bell chimes
the half-hour,
sometimes.

2

Sometimes night falls
in this whitewashed room
below the volcano.

A ceiling fan swirls
the salt breezes wafting
through the open window.

Like clotted cream
in pooled starlight, jasmine
edges the path to my door.

The volcano, tuxedo black,
escorts the satin moon
into a night sky
sated with stars
that seem so much closer here.

Cicadas chisel
the silence.

I lie still

and sense the trace
of a trace,
the whispers of lives
not quite remembered,

knowing the volcano pulses
with molten rock
from Earth's first days;

rising, it poured crimson
through fissures in the thin skin,
flaming streams now
obsidian rock,
jet, sparkling.

At first light, the lip
of the volcano summons
me from sleep.

Breathless,
I rush outside, half-dressed,
drawn to its crest.

Dawn's Song

Form from light,
form from air,

in a hush
expectant

as the moment
before creation.

Sugarcane stalks rustle
in gusts of wind,
heralding birdsong.

Two lavender peaks
scale a watermelon sky.

From the golden womb
of the sun, day is born.

Guzzle

A steep laneway clambers
up to a small white house
with a sea-blue floor.

At six in the morning,
I awaken to a rooster
trumpeting the new day's
rising heat.

Midday, louvres angled,
the slender streets lie
empty but for a few cats
asleep on sizzling stones.

Evening's breeze tumbles
down the hillside
and in through the open door

I inhale, guzzling
the cool air.

Finally, heatstruck,
I take the footpath
to the woods and fall
senseless into deep, dry grass.

The alabaster moon floats
in the dark arc of the sky,
a lantern strung
between two ebony peaks
and the platinum sea.

Ignite

I drift through the brine,
porous as pumice stone,
sea salt scouring my body,
old skins shed

as the island's silhouette
disappears in a riddle of haze,
reappears, disappears

Gliding on a thermal updraft,
sinew and bone
turn buoyant as air

Supine on moist sand,
my spine curves
to meet the lissom Earth

Kindled by a tangelo sun,
I ignite
into life

Chimera

In caramel heat,
my eyelids flutter
and close,
flutter
and open.

The air animates, quivering
like thousands of invisible wings.
Solid hillsides heave.

The volcano, a creature asleep
on its belly, stretches out
along the centre of the island —

its snout rises in razor-sharp line from the sea
to a long, sinewy neck and broad scaly back,
to a hump, near the last third of the island's diameter,
that dips to a knobby tail falling straight onto a rock beach below,
where it lies trapped under mounds of scree.

Bulging muscled flanks and legs
thrust the hooves down into surrounding lowlands,
straining, but failing to stand upright
in their cage of earth and stone.

The beast pushes its tail against the beach rocks,
flings them aside, raises its tail high in the air,
slaps it down, lashing the sea, churning colossal waves

that come crashing back
against the island's shores, headlands and lowlands,
shattering earth and stone.

Unshackled,
up on all fours, unsteady
at first,

he stares at me
wistfully

baying
a guttural
greeting.

Spellbound

Through tall grass to the world's edge,
I walk where coastline careens
to a restive sea below
the volcano, that hulk fuming
against a torch red sundown.

I climb its black back,
my feet trembling
on the cone of tuff and cinder,
the smoke curling
from earthen fissures,

and from the volcano's peak,
javelins of flame pierce
the sable sky, firing
smoky clouds fluorescent orange.

I lay my body
on rocky soil, transfixed
by the luminous heavens,
when a wayward star
plummets past me, blazing
a blue-white trail to the sea.

Like a brass key cut
for a steel lock,
he approaches me,
hazel eyes velvet,
horse-like nostrils flared,

he strokes my shoulder
with small, insistent breaths.

My breasts swell,
their flesh electric.
Blood unleashes
charged particles that circuit
from him through me
and back through him,

each entry to my body
drawing inward,
clenching,
quivering,
opening,

till, deep in the recesses
of my core,
a rusty latch
unlocks.

Stay up here with me
all night, here on the edge
of the world.

Seamless

His chest and head rise
seamless from my hips

and when I lift
myself up
so we're eye to eye

we fit
like a centaur,

our torso
tapering to
muscled haunches
on four thrashing legs.

And from our throat,
somewhere between
animal and human,

a feral wail —
lament of our pain,
howl of our rapture.

Cistern

He takes pleasure
in my skin
my smell
my taste.

He gazes inside me,
taps the vein
to ancient springs cloistered
in the pear-shaped cistern
of my body.

The living current starts
where he touches.

Fulcrum

You gather me in your arms
so swiftly, so tightly,

I cannot
breathe.

This moment
comes first —

the fulcrum of the flesh wins over
the life of the mind.

The Clock

Beloved,
my bed is a huge clock

and we, its human hands
joined at the centre.

Inside me, you trace the angles
all around the dial.

I am your day,
you are my night.

Your night,
my day.

Opal

The neighbouring island broods
grey and rocky, sea and sky fused

morning sun wrapped in haze, ochre
fruit swaddled in gauze

At midday, wide panels of light break
from pewter clouds, pour
into the slate sea, coalesce

into a mercury band racing
across the horizon

At sunset, the nearby island sails
on glistening seas, an opal
set in gold.

Toffee

My limbs sprawled across the bow
of your old wooden boat, sunlight
butters my skin.

You add brown sugar to my syrup,
bring me to the boil,
stir until fully melted.

I awake in the night
to a sweet ache,
like warm, stretched toffee

in the opening
between my thighs.

Green Kimono

Shedding our clothes
to the beat, we dance

in a darkened room to French music
from a cheap radio,

the world far away.

You drape me
in a green kimono adorned
with orange and red flowers.

Your hands slide in
through side openings,
caress curves and hollows.

The kimono never
comes off.

Wheelbarrow

My night visitor,

you grab me
from behind,

hold me high
like a wheelbarrow,
my hips the handles,

push me across the bed,
my nipples just grazing
the linen sheet.

Each Time

You lift me weightless
when I am careworn,

remain still
when I take charge,

hold me snugly
when I feel restless,

rock me
when I feel small.

Each time anew
you make me new.

FLIGHT

We soar currents of air
like two gulls —

on rising
the glowing white of my belly,

on falling
the blackness of your wings.

Of all the ways you have touched me

it will surprise you
but I loved most

the time we walked hand-in-hand
up the hill to a village concert,

our way strewn with fresh magenta
petals from the bougainvillea hedge.

Piano music floated down to us
through narrow, cobbled streets.

As we sat in makeshift seats,
swallows scythed over our heads

while you stroked the curve
at the nape of my neck

in time
with the legato.

Long Night

Storm warning.
It is time to leave.

All night long, the wind
wails, moans,

pleads,

while tree branches whipsaw
against blackness,

the volcano a point
of stillness.

On the last ferry out,
the island ebbing,

she sobs scalding tears,
doesn't know why,

her need to cry
knowledge enough.

III

And it was then

the flame inside you stood straight up,
tall, gold-coloured; and your heart walked forward
easily, as though something had called it, laid itself
on the anvil of that silence.

— from "Music and Silence: Seven Variations"
Jan Zwicky

Shadow

The afternoon before I left the island, I sat dreamily at the sea's edge, shielded from the agitated surf behind a waist-high boulder, the sun toasting my skin, the waves licking my toes. A massive breaker reared up, tracking straight towards me. Mesmerized, unable to move as cold salty water crashed over me, I gulped for air, the sea swallowed my left arm, tugged your amulet off my wrist. Now, months later, my arm remains bare, the feel of your silver band lingers there, a shadow on my skin.

Rush of the Wind

Under twisted olive branches
we took shelter from sudden rain

while, high above us on the mountainside,
the small white house stood empty.

Deep silence waits there now
in the rush of the wind,

whistling through two round windows
and arched sea-blue door.

Top to Tail

A beach of ash grey and magenta rocks scrabbled from the sandstone cliff, rocks pummelled smooth by the surge of cerulean sea… Face down, my arm torqued to line up sun-fired rocks along my spine, from top to tail. The weight of cloud and sky pressed down against vertebrae as Earth's crust heaved up against my belly: minerals filled cellular spaces and crystallized, my body preserved as living fossil.

Bowl

An orange crescent moon
vibrates in starless night:
slice of cantaloupe
in a black glass bowl.

Scent of Jasmine

Alone, in humid night air
beneath a ceiling fan,
I traced my body
with a jasmine flower.

~

My skin the perfume he scented,
the scent lingering there
for days, testimonial
to first touch.

~

I look at my body and imagine,
imagine his desire looking back at me,
his desire
my desire now — my self.

Compass

A tangled undergrowth of twisted roots and gnarled stems grew untended between us. On that impassable ground, I tripped and fell, rose and fell again. You had vanished. Yet each time I rose, I listened for the cadence of your walk. Now you dance to a new jazz rhythm, luring me to your breath in hushed night, clearing the path to you, new woman.

Gently Down

She returns home
sleek and strange.

Compelled,
he lifts her in his arms

as if she were a child,
sponges her skin with lavender water.

Afterwards, he slips a silk gown
over her head, lays her

gently down
and sits beside her,

his hand clasping hers.
She smiles, tentative.

At daybreak, they open their eyes
to see winter's sky

don a scarlet coat

New Clothes

I lie face down on our bed,
ready for sleep,

she climbs on and
blankets me naked,

her breasts flatten
to right and left of my spine,

her arms are sleeves
for my arms

her fingers gloves
for my fingers

her feet slippers
for my feet,

her wedge of dark curls
scrubs against my buttocks,

her body clothes
my skin.

I roll over
inside my new clothes
to feel her curls
tangle over my hard

and it begins
again.

CHANT

My body is antique satin, you the tailor
drape me even or uneven;

my body is gold, you the artisan
melt me molten, form me;

my body is rosewood, you the carver
chisel me, polish me;

my body is glass, you the glass blower
shape me, dissolve me with your breath;

my body, the rudder, you the helmsman
chart my passage.

ENTRUSTED

Nestled like silver spoons,
we usher in the day,
hip entrusted to hip.

Late afternoon,
I am your finger puppet, ruled
by your hand.

At day's end, I unfurl
over you
like a spring fern.

In deepest night,
our bodies twist
against a knotted rope,

tumbling
towards
unknown places.

Boldly

Let's make love
after we clean the house.

Let's see if we have energy,
after we pay all the bills.

I can't make love now,
I have work to do.

No
more.
Boldly

kiss me in the car
when the windows fog over with rain.

Madly undress me on the floor
the moment I walk in the door.

Leave dinner
on the stove.

Life Mate

Flash of brilliant crimson
in the snowy reaches
of apple-green cedar bushes.

A glowing, black-bearded
cardinal and his paler mate
are dining out today
at our bird feeder,

perched together,
side by side,
pecking at the seed.

He turns towards her,
places a kernel
inside her mouth.

She flies off.

He follows.

Autumn Angles

Their house sits back from the city sidewalk,
under orange and garnet leaves
clinging sparsely to autumn's skeleton.

Tall, slim and bespectacled, his bent
back twists to the right, arms stiff
with effort, as in slow motion he drags

his rake through damp
layers of leathery leaves, clumping
them into small

mounds. His wife, torso still
straight, hovers, shovel ready
to gather the harvest.

Does she imagine him as he was, raking
with vigour? Then, could she have
pictured him now?

He tires, she shifts closer,
eases the rake from him,
wordless, completes his portion.

Head drooped, he regains
breath, reclaims his rake,
begins again.

~

Last year, I found three grey hairs
in my eyebrows, slightly puckered
skin in my elbow's crook.

Time wears more lightly
on you: a mere crease
between your cheek and ear.

Our bodies tilt
at different angles
towards the burning leaves.

At the Window

A middle-aged couple, we gaze out
our living room window,

my face pressed
against the cool pane.

You tenderize
my earlobe,

hike up my skirt, drop it down
over our hips

and slide into me.

Once again, nerve endings shiver
all through my body

as two silver shadows
slow-tango

across the vinyl siding
of the house next door.

Blue Branches

Moments before moonrise,
our bodies mingle
with the growing shadows,

our laughter skims
the low fog,

we float upwards,

two fireflies
illuminating

the blue branches
of midnight.

BEAT

A fresh wind propels me
down a maple-lined path,
autumn's amber leaves oscillate
in the breeze, their veins gilded with light

Crumpled leaves fallen to ground
cavort with each other, caper
across gleaming grass, caress
a tree trunk twisted into human form

while in feathered queues
lime-green bushes bend as one
to an unseen hand

And my heart beats

Acknowledgements

Thank you to all those whose insights and support contributed to this book's evolution: Joan Baril, Sheila Baslaw, Michele Caruso, Pauline Comeau, Claudia Coutu Radmore, Barry Dempster, Marcello D'Amico, Laura Etherden, Fabiola Famularo, Ted Fryia, Adele Graf, Elyse Hynes, Rod Pederson, Clara Rametta, Peter Richardson, Nate Simpson, Dean Steadman, Carol Stephen, Lesley Strutt and JC Sulzenko. Thanks, as well, to everyone at the 2011 Banff Centre Writing Studio, where my participation was made possible by the Ontario Artists Fund.

For their wisdom and editorial assistance on earlier portions of this book and another manuscript currently in progress, I am grateful to John Barton, Karen Connelly, Michael Dennis, Carolyn Forché, Daphne Marlatt, Susan McMaster, Stuart Ross, Olive Senior, D.M. Thomas and Jan Zwicky.

I count myself fortunate to be involved with Ottawa's Tree Reading Series, which opened the doors of poetry for me, and where I found many friendships.

A selection of poems, from an early draft of the manuscript which became *Ignite,* was published in Canada by Bondi Studios as a chapbook illustrated by Australian artist Marcello D'Amico under the title *Cistern of my Body,* and in Australia by Aeolian Press.

Earlier versions of some of the poems in this book were published in *Vallum, Bywords* and the *Maple Tree Literary Supplement* as well as in several collaborative chapbooks. I also thank the John Newlove Award for selecting an earlier version of "Burnt Forest" for honourable mention.

I am indebted to George Payerle, whose sensitive editing of this book heard more than the words on the page and added depth and clarity to the poems. And, my warmest appreciation to Karen Haughian, publisher of Signature Editions, and her excellent team, for bringing *Ignite* into the world.

My abiding love to Brian Tannenbaum, my husband, whose unconditional love and support sustains me.

About the Author

Born and raised in Montreal, Quebec, Rona Shaffran lives in Ottawa, Ontario. She recently retired as co-director of the Tree Reading Series, one of Canada's longest running poetry venues, where she is also a member of the board of directors and organizes master poetry workshops. Rona Shaffran is a graduate of the Humber School for Writers and the Banff Centre Writing Studio. Her poems have appeared in Canadian literary journals, including *Vallum*, in an illustrated chapbook published and distributed in Canada and Australia, and in several collaborative chapbooks. She has won honourable mention for the John Newlove Poetry Award. Retired several years ago from federal government work, Rona has chaired the boards and committees of many non-profit organizations. She devotes time to writing and to travel, and is at work on a second manuscript that includes both poetry and prose. *Ignite* is her first published book of poetry.

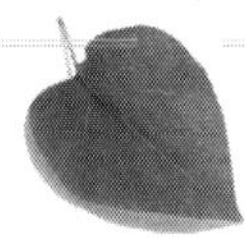

Eco-Audit
Printing this book using Rolland Opaque 50 instead of virgin fibres paper saved the following resources:

Trees	Solid Waste	Water	Air Emissions
1	75 kg	2,481 L	230 kg